This book belongs to:

Brimming with creative inspiration, how-to projects, and useful information to enrich your everyday life, Quarto Knows is a favorite destination for those pursuing their interests and passions. Visit our site and dig deeper with our books into your area of interest: Quarto Creates, Quarto Cooks, Quarto Homes, Quarto Lives, Quarto Drives, Quarto Explores, Quarto Gifts, or Quarto Kids.

First published in 2011 by Walter Foster Jr., an imprint of The Quarto Group.
26391 Crown Valley Parkway, Suite 220, Mission Viejo, CA 92691, USA.
T (949) 380-7510 **F** (949) 380-7575 **www.QuartoKnows.com**

ISBN: 978-1-60058-226-4

Drawing steps by Russell Farrell
"Window Garden" and "Horse Bandana" crafts by Megan Friday
Step-by-step craft illustrations by Diana Fisher

Printed in China
20 19 18 17 16

MIX
Paper from responsible sources
FSC® C016973
FSC www.fsc.org

I ♥ Horses!

Activity Book

Giddy-up great stickers, trivia, step-by-step drawing projects, and more for the horse lover in you!

Table of Contents

Horse Breeds

There are many different types of horses. Turn the page to see what is special and unique about each breed.

Horse Breeds

American Quarter Horse

Dutch Warmblood

American Saddlebred

Hanoverian

Arabian

Friesian

Appaloosa

Hackney Horse

Highland Pony

Morgan

Lipizzaner

Palomino

Norwegian Fjord Pony

Mustang

Paso Fino

Percheron

Pinto

Pony of the Americas

Shetland Pony

Shire

Thoroughbred

Rocky Mountain Pony

Welsh Mountain Pony

Tennessee Walking Horse

Drawing Projects

Learn how to draw 16 different horse breeds by starting with basic shapes and then following step by simple step. Practice your drawings on scrap paper. Once you've mastered each breed, you can add a finished colored drawing to the Sketch Pad beginning on page 79.

Getting Started

When you look closely at the drawings in this book, you'll notice that they're made up of basic shapes, such as circles, ovals, and triangles. To draw all your favorite horses, just start with simple shapes as you see here. It's easy and fun!

Circles are one way to start a horse's head, chest, and hips.

Ovals make good profile heads and muzzles.

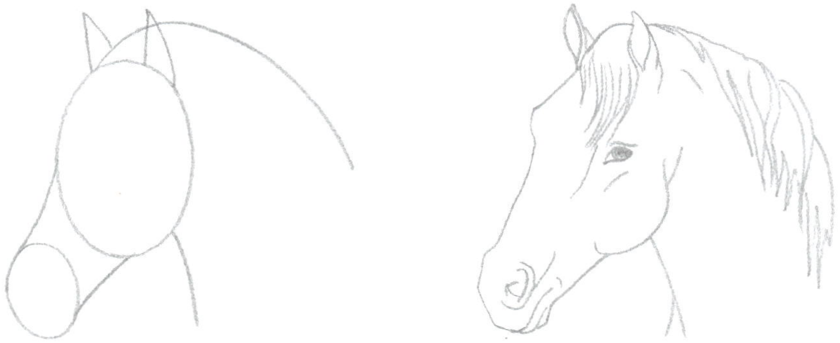

Triangles are perfect for upright ears!

Coloring Tips

There's more than one way to bring your four-legged friends to life on paper—you can use crayons, markers, or colored pencils. Just be sure you have plenty of good "horse colors"—black, brown, and white, plus yellow, orange, red, and blue.

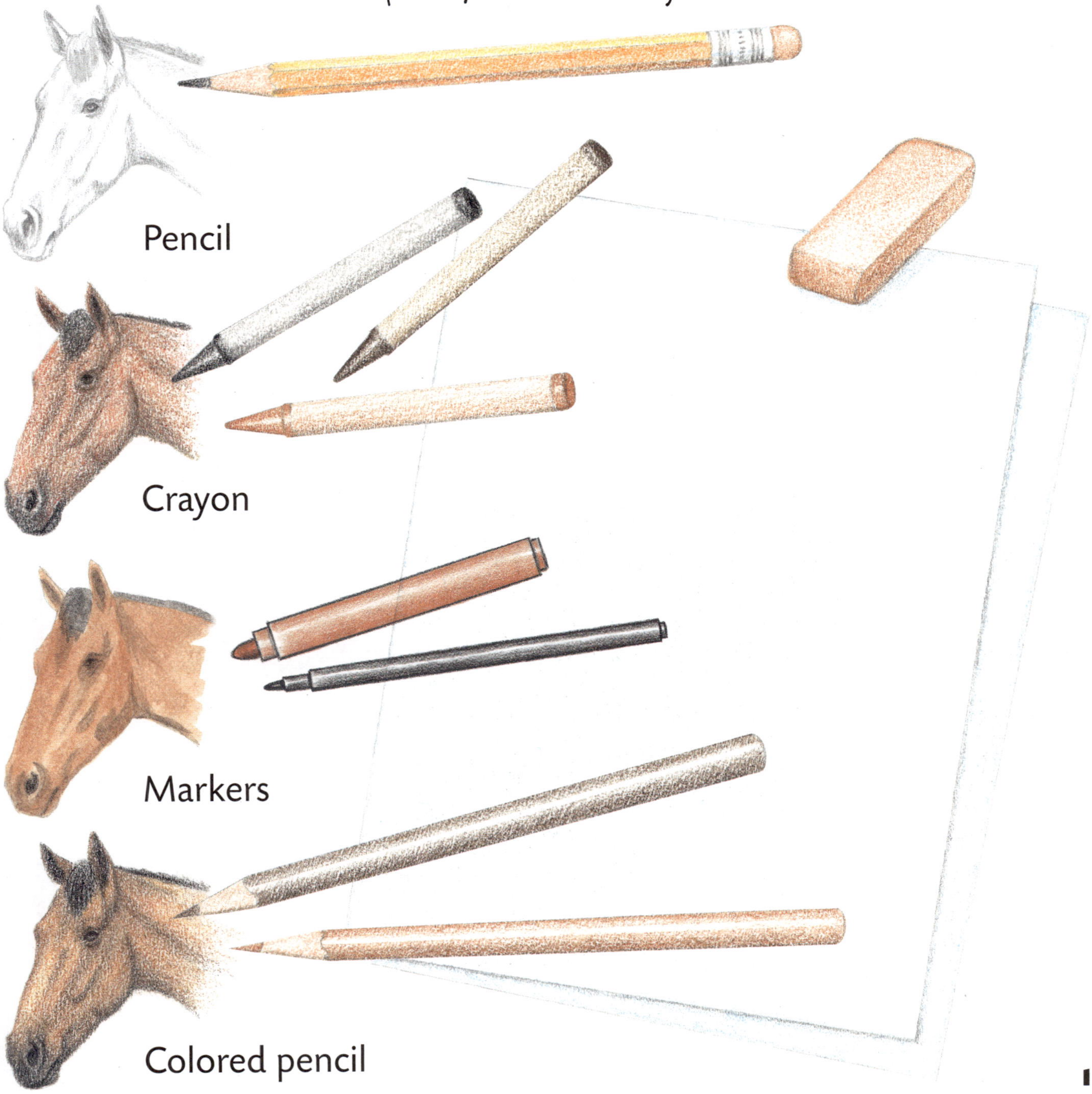

Hackney Horse

This handsome show horse is strutting its stuff—stretch out those legs and arch that tail high!

1

2

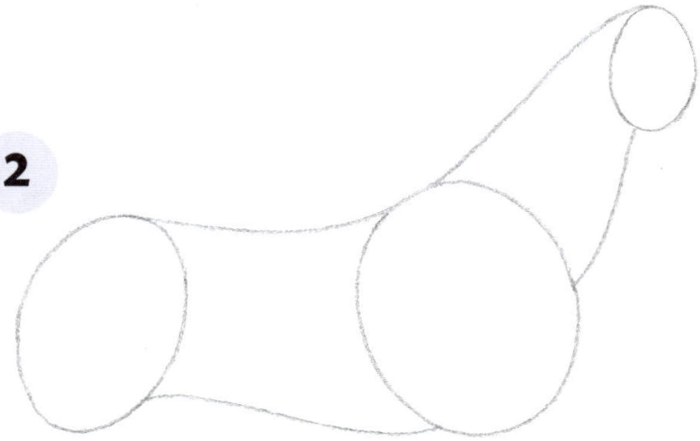

3

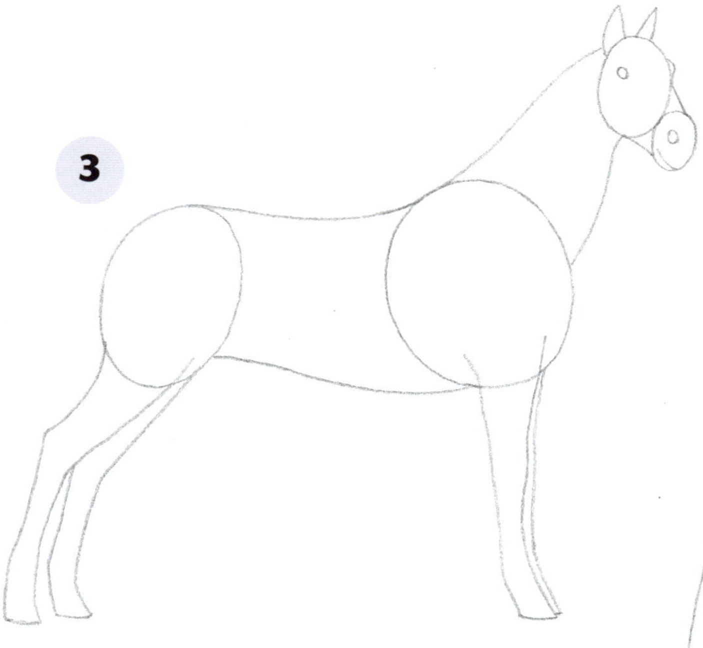

4

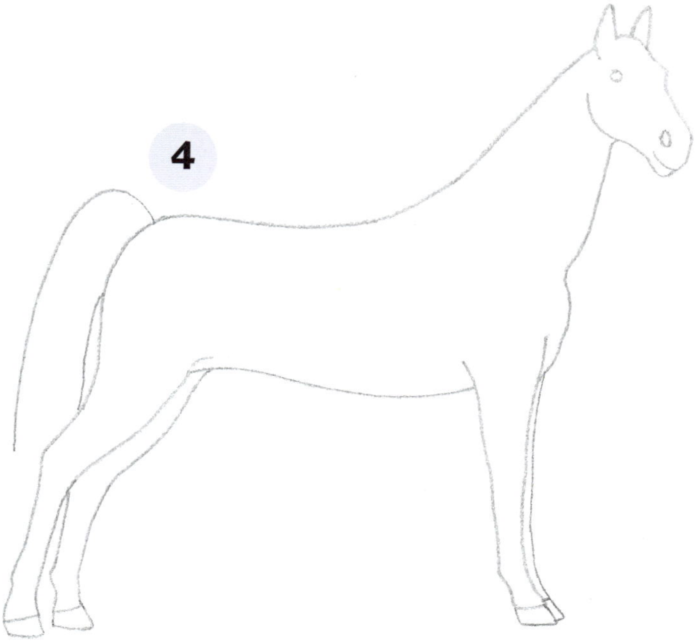

5

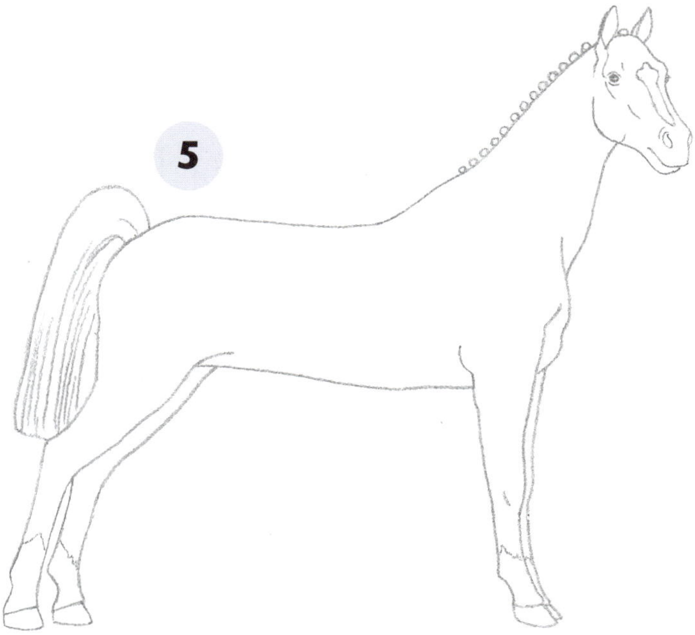

6

Pinto

This color breed has a cool patterned coat that sets it apart! A Quarter Horse or Thoroughbred Pinto can also be called a "Paint."

1

2

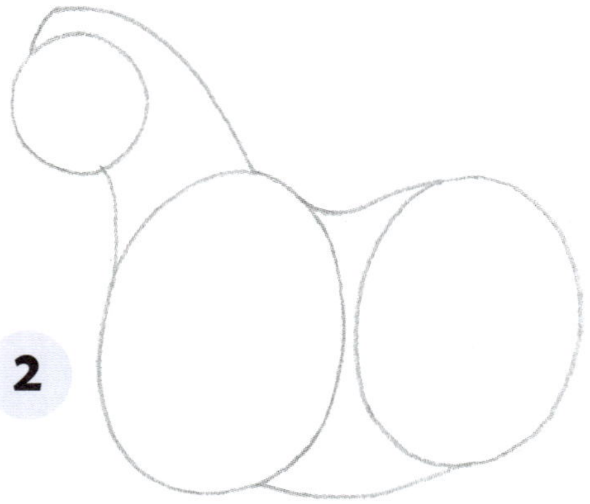

3

4

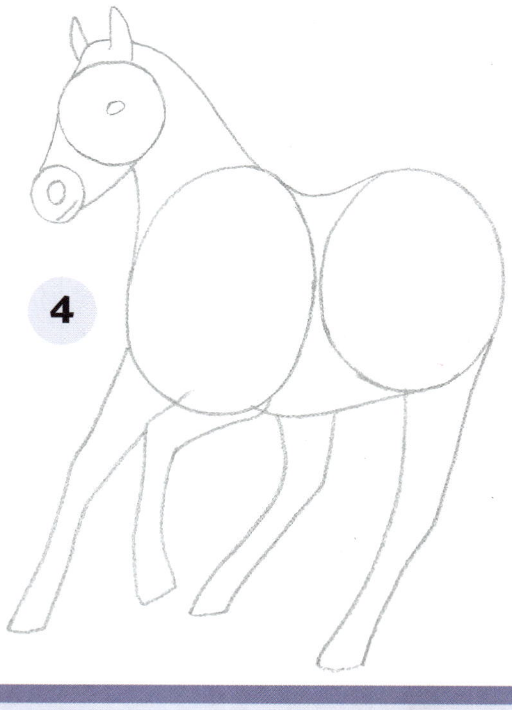

Fun Fact

Both Pintos and Paints have the same patterns of coloring, so how can you tell the difference between these breeds? Every Paint is a Pinto, but not every Pinto is a Paint. The Pinto registry is less exclusive than the Paint registry.

6

5

7

Noriker

An ancient Austrian draft breed (heavy workhorse), the Noriker is strong and stocky, with a long silky mane, tail, and forelock.

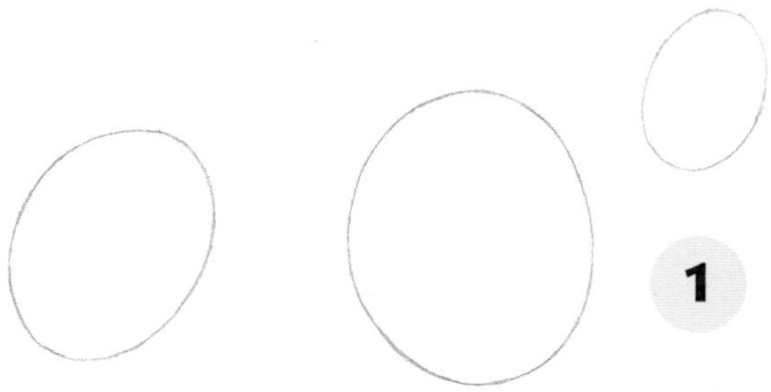

1

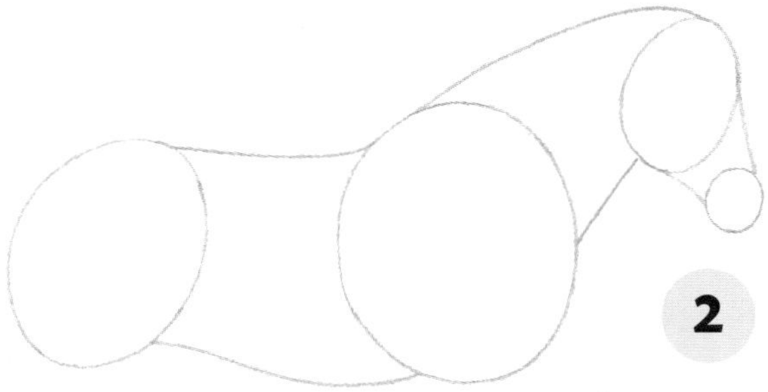

2

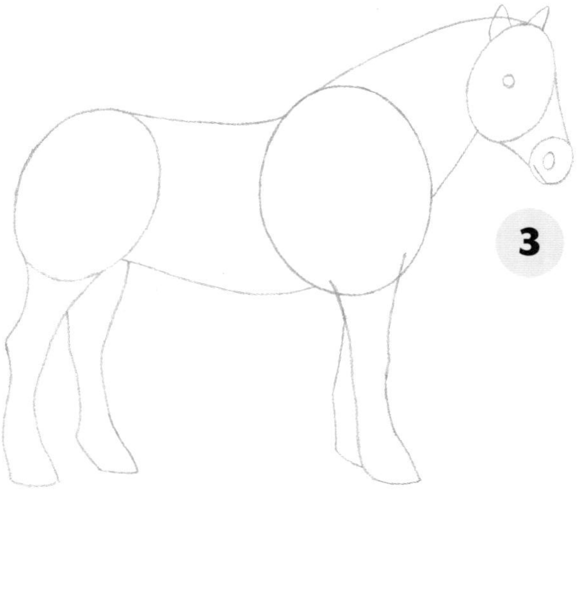

3

4

5

6

Hanoverian Foal

Start this long-legged baby with two circles
for the body. Then finish with a short, brushlike tail
and a stiff, upright mane.

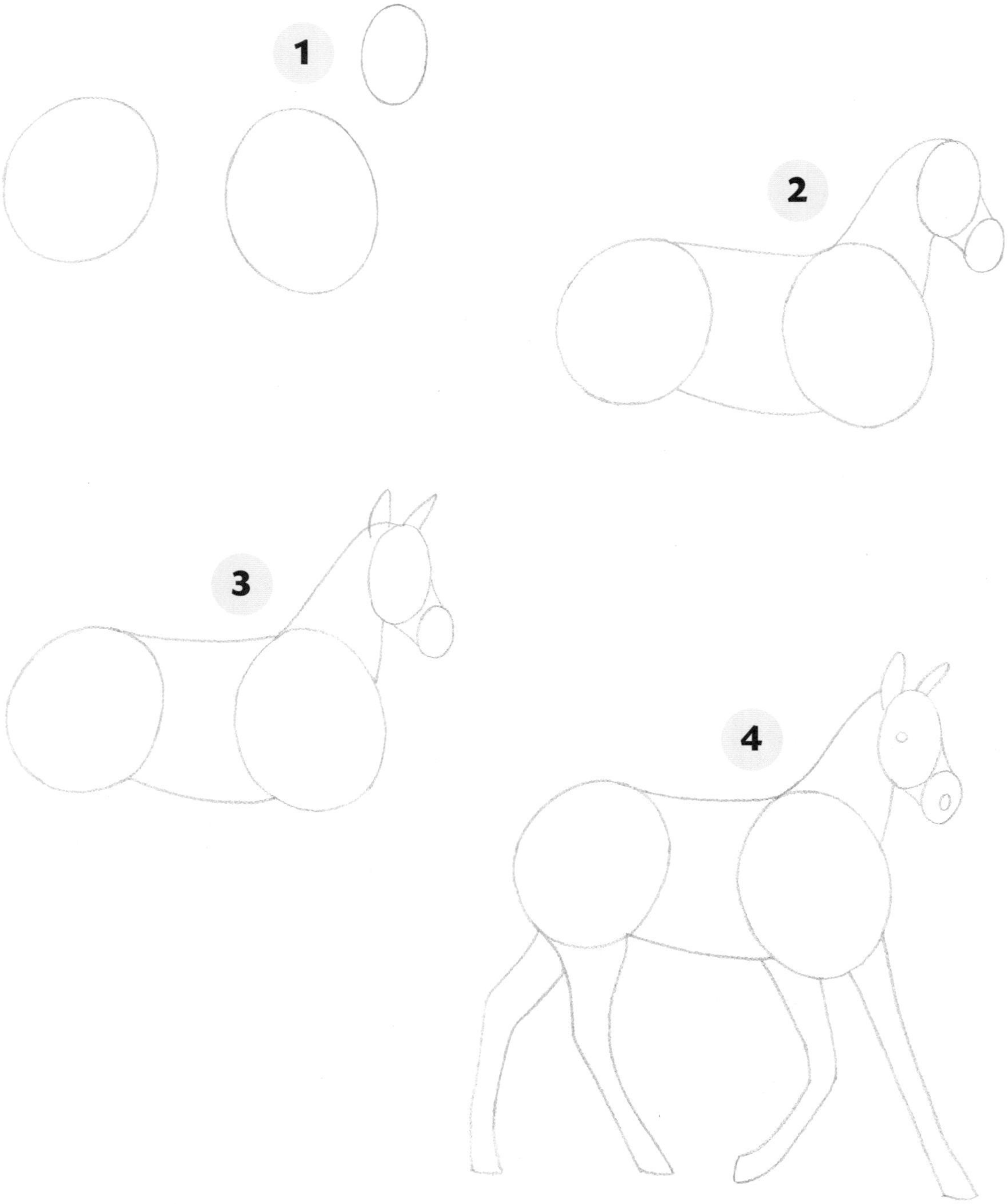

5

6

7

Fun Fact

The first Hanoverians worked as carriage and military horses. But the Hanoverian is now one of the most important sport horse breeds. With their long stride, powerful action, and excellent jumping skills, they have won many world championships, including a number of Olympic medals and more World Cups than any other breed!

Morgan

Small but super strong and hardy, the Morgan has a draft horse's muscular hindquarters but thinner legs and an elegant face.

1

2

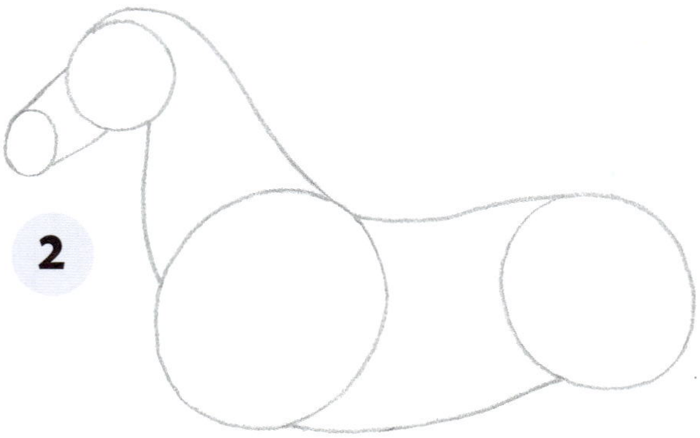

3

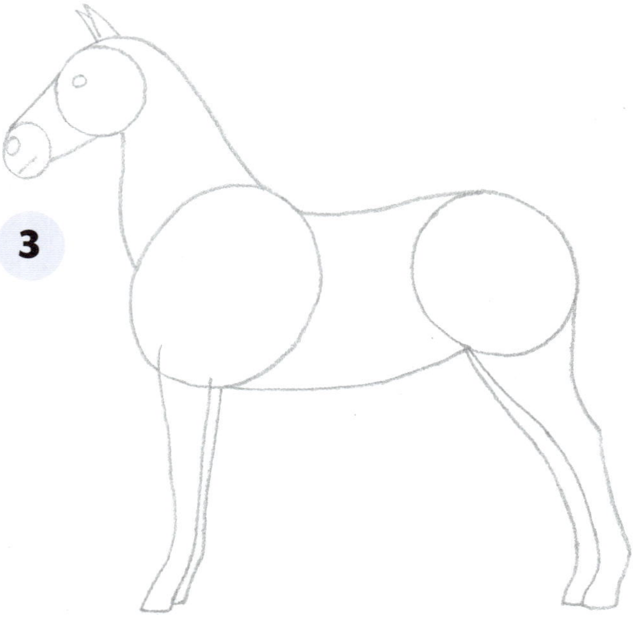

4

5

6

Thoroughbred

The fastest breed in the world, the athletic and courageous Thoroughbred can run and jump for miles and miles!

1

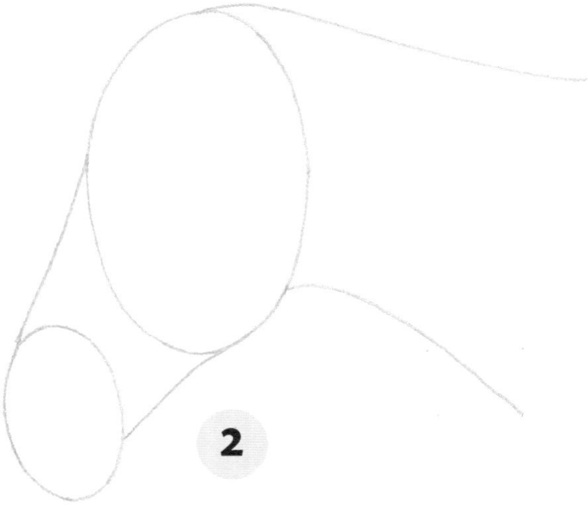

2

3

4

5

Fun Fact

Every Thoroughbred racehorse celebrates its birthday on New Year's Day. A newborn is considered a foal until January 1st of the year after it is born; then it's called a "yearling."

Clydesdale

The Clydesdale is a big and powerful draft horse, with long leg hairs—called "feathers"—that almost cover its hooves!

5

6

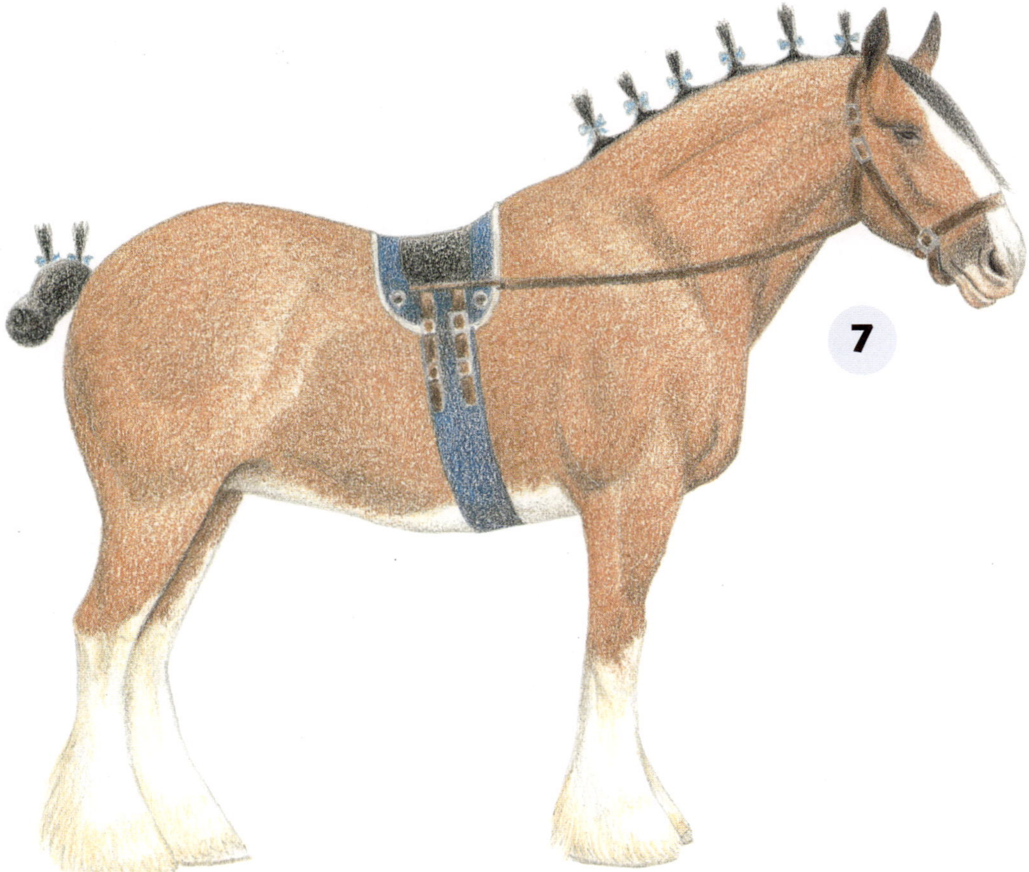

7

Kathiawari

This narrowly built horse from India has distinctive ears that curve inward until their tips actually touch!

1

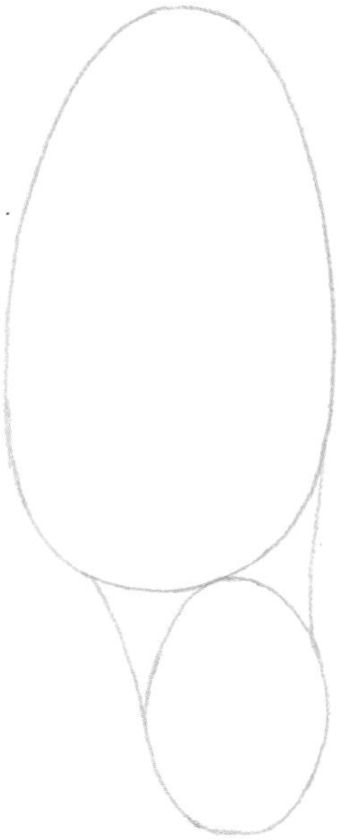

2

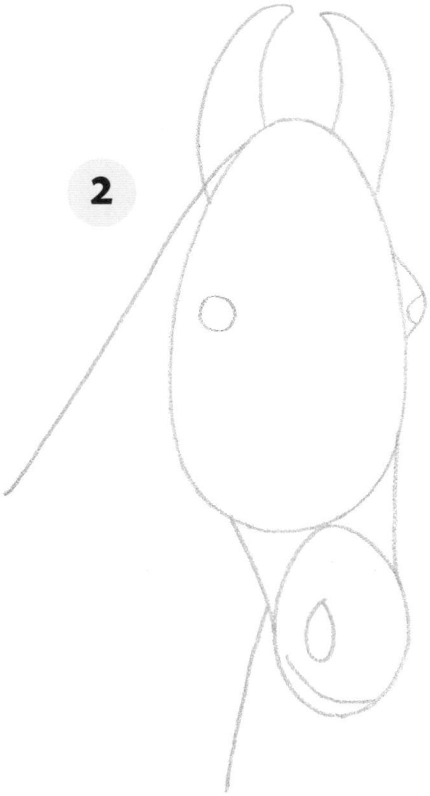

3

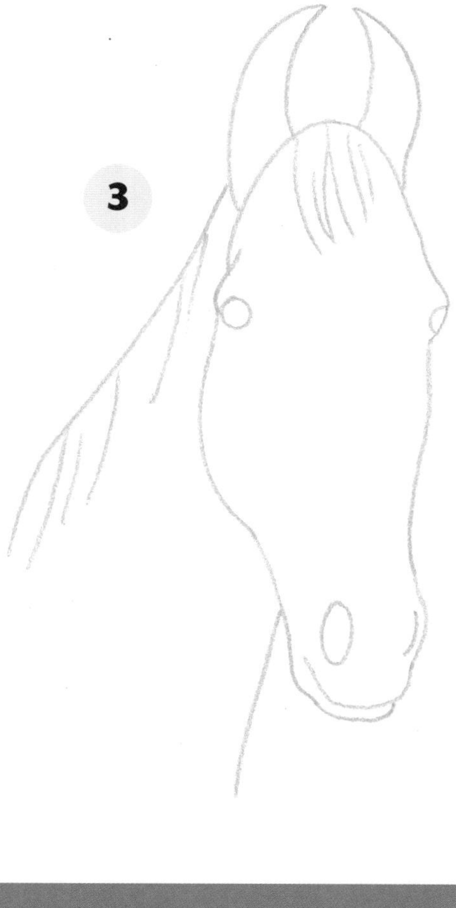

4

5

Fun Fact

This horse is small, but it's also tough, which is why the Kathiawari is a favorite of tent-pegging athletes. Originally a way to practice wild boar hunting, *tent pegging* is now a popular sport in India. To play the game, an athlete rides to the center of an arena and, while on horseback, uses the tip of a lance to pick up a small wooden block—or peg. Picking up the peg earns the rider half a point; picking up the peg and carrying it to the opposite corner of the arena earns a full point.

Shetland Pony

A favorite breed of pony-loving kids, the adorable Shetland is tiny but tough, with a round belly and short, stocky legs.

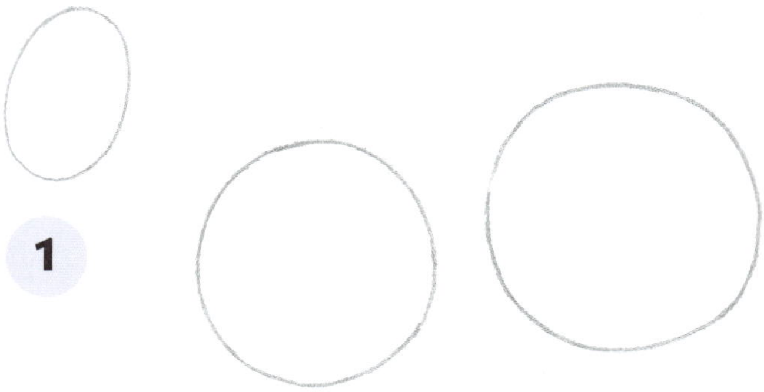

1

2

3

4

5

American Saddlebred

This high-spirited horse shows off its proud style with a high-flying tail and a prancing step!

1

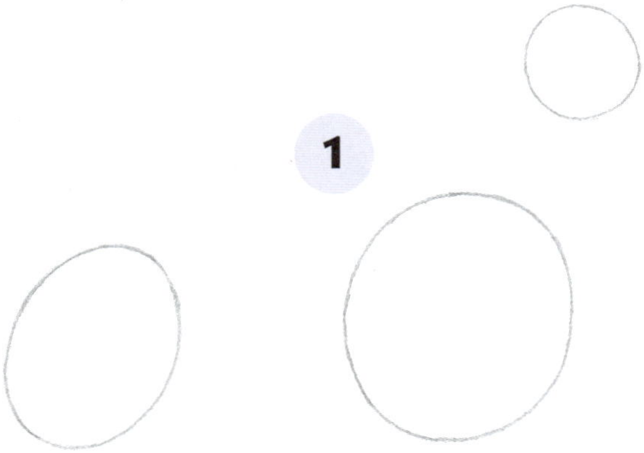

2

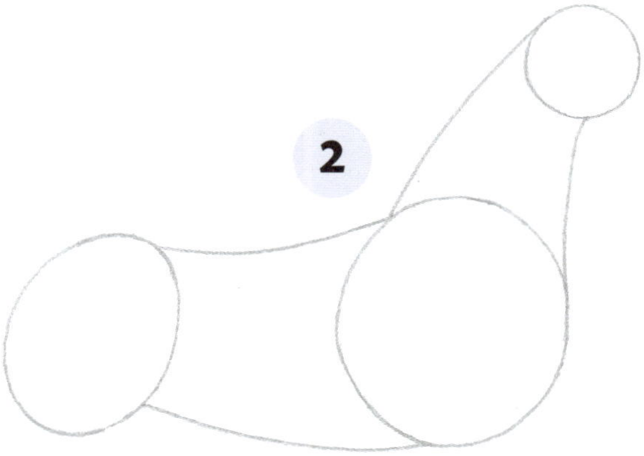

3

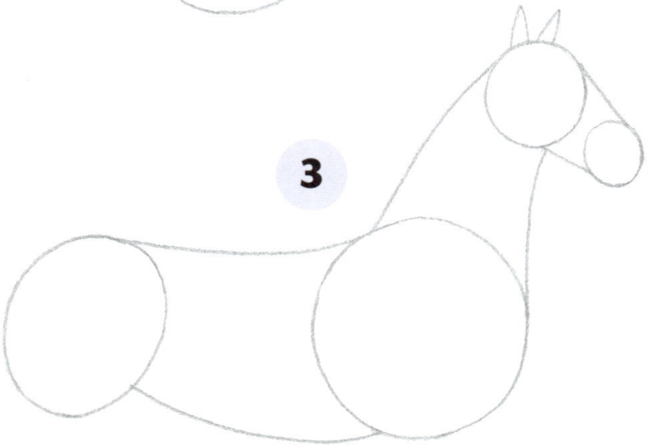

4

Fun Fact

The Saddlebred not only walks, trots, and canters—it can also perform two additional smooth, easy-riding gaits: *slow gait* and *rack*. Some horses can carry out the five gaits naturally at birth, but others must be trained to perform the two special gaits.

5

6

7

Pony of the Americas

This polka-dotted pony has a two-toned mane and a long, arched neck. Draw its spotted coat with circles and ovals.

1

2

Fun Fact

In 1954, an Iowan breeder named Les Boomhower discovered the unique coat of a foal born with an Arab/Appaloosa mother and a Shetland father. This foal was the first Pony of the Americas, a breed developed for children to show and ride.

3

4

5

Tennessee Walking Horse

With its ultra-smooth walk, this gaited horse is a proud show-ring competitor with a sweet, gentle personality.

1

2

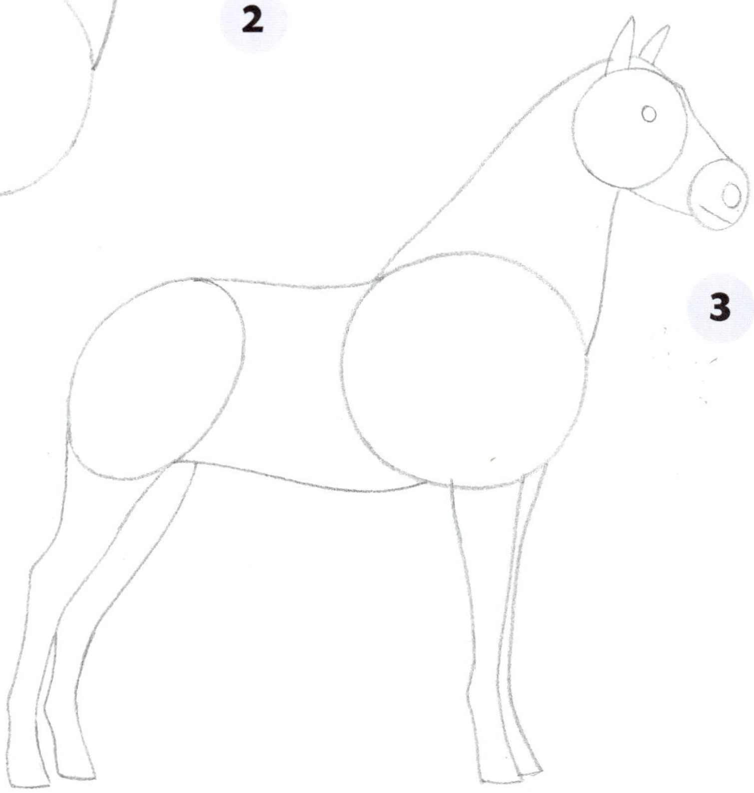

3

4

5

6

American Quarter Horse

With its muscular hindquarters and powerful shoulders, this Western horse can sprint like an Olympian and stop on a dime!

1

2

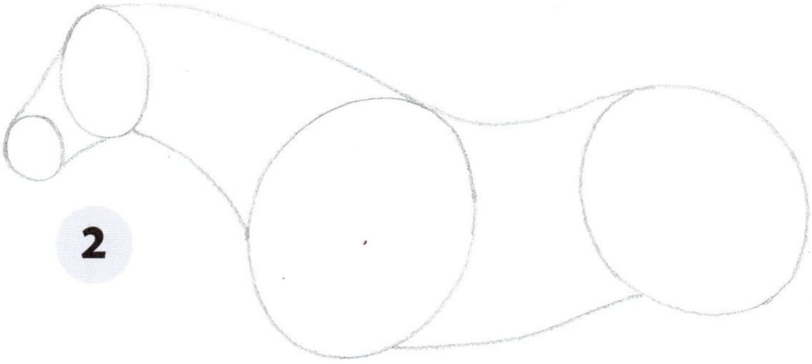

3

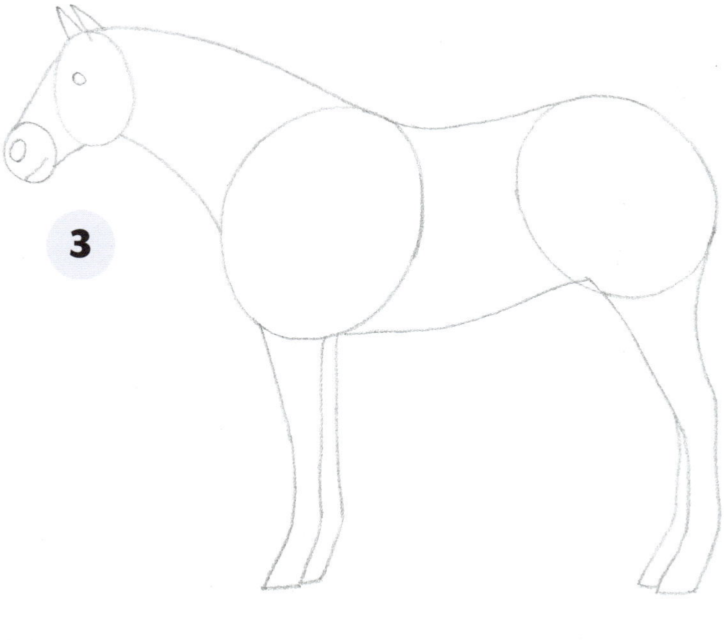

Fun Fact

The traditional choice for cowboys—both on the ranch and on TV—the American Quarter Horse has always been popular. Now it's the #1 breed worldwide, with more than 3 million entries in the American Quarter Horse Association registry!

4

5

6

Highland Pony

This sure-footed Scottish pony has the build of a draft horse, with soft, silky feathers on its lower legs.

1

2

3

4

5

Fun Fact

Highland foals often have "primitive" markings on their coats, including stripes on the back, shoulders, and legs; or dark spots on the mane, tail, and legs. Some of the markings fade over time, but others continue to show throughout the ponies' entire lives.

Paso Fino

Also called a "stepping" horse for its natural, lively gait, the Paso Fino has long hind legs and pasterns and very flexible joints.

4

5

6

Arabian

Its delicate, dished profile; large eyes and nostrils; and small, pointed ears give the Arabian a noble and gentle appearance.

Horse Crafts

Get out your scissors and glue—it's time to stop horsing around and start doing some good deeds for your favorite steed. These creature creations will put a giant smile on any horse.

Window Garden

Create a fabulous garden full of fresh, homegrown delights for your favorite friend in the stable.

Materials

- Bucket (galvanized steel or aluminum)
- Hammer
- Nail
- Scissors
- Paintbrush
- Enough fabric to wrap around the bucket 1¼ times
- Outdoor decoupage
- Trim
- Craft glue
- Potting soil
- Seeds: wheatgrass, carrots, or radishes

Have an adult help you use the hammer and nail to poke a few drain holes into the bottom of the bucket by gently tapping the nail through in several spots.

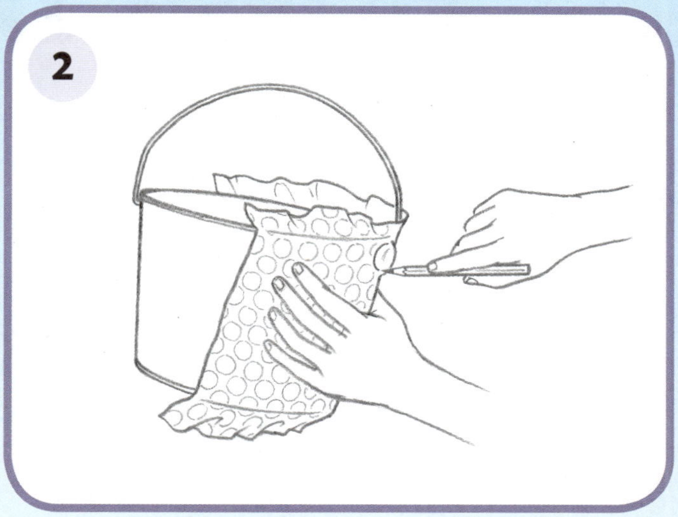

Cover the exterior of the bucket with fabric by measuring and trimming two pieces that each cover ¾ of the bucket's outer surface. Cut holes for the handles.

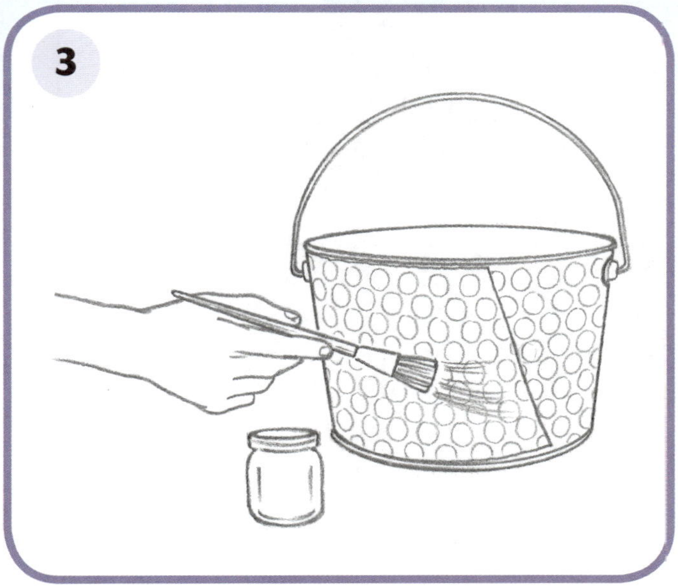

Use a paintbrush to coat the bucket with outdoor decoupage, affix one piece of fabric to the bucket, and then cover it with another layer of decoupage. Repeat this step with the other piece of fabric overlapping the first piece. Let the bucket dry overnight. Apply two more coats of decoupage, allowing it to dry for 15 minutes between coats.

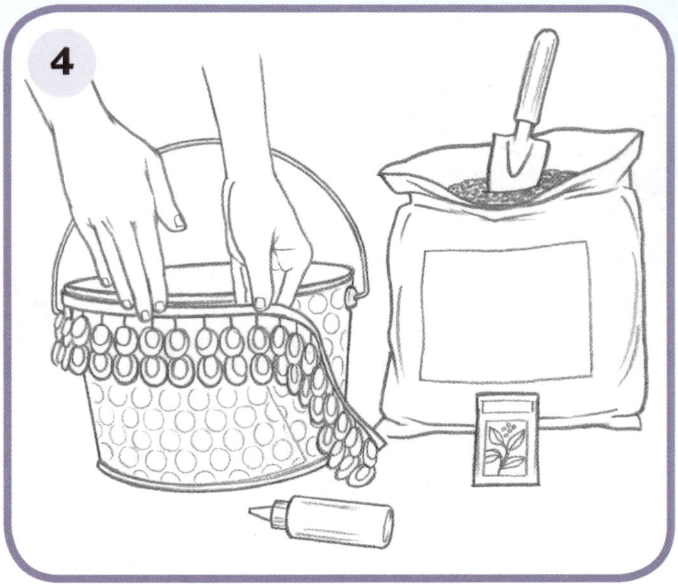

When the fabric is completely dry, use craft glue to attach trim around the perimeter of the bucket's top edge. Again, let the bucket dry overnight. Fill the bucket with potting soil and plant the seeds of your choice. Keep the soil moist until the seeds sprout. Place the garden in a sunny window and water it regularly as the plant grows.

Horse Bandana

Accessorize your animal pal with custom-made style.

Materials

- A square piece of fabric with sides equal to the distance around your horse's neck
- Iron-on letters
- Iron
- Trim
- Craft glue
- Tracing paper or photocopier (optional)
- Pencil or white pencil/crayon
- Fabric paint
- Jewels (optional)
- Ruler
- Scissors

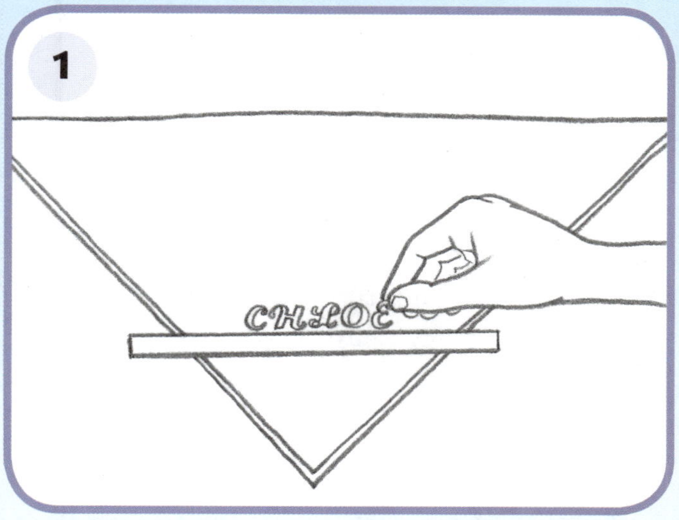

◀ Have an adult measure your horse's neck and help you measure and cut the square piece of fabric. Then fold your bandana to form a triangle. You can personalize the size and look to match to your horse's size and personality. Lay out your pet's name with iron-on letters so that it fits above the tip of your bandana. Use a ruler or straight edge to space the letters evenly. Have an adult iron them onto the bandana according to the package instructions.

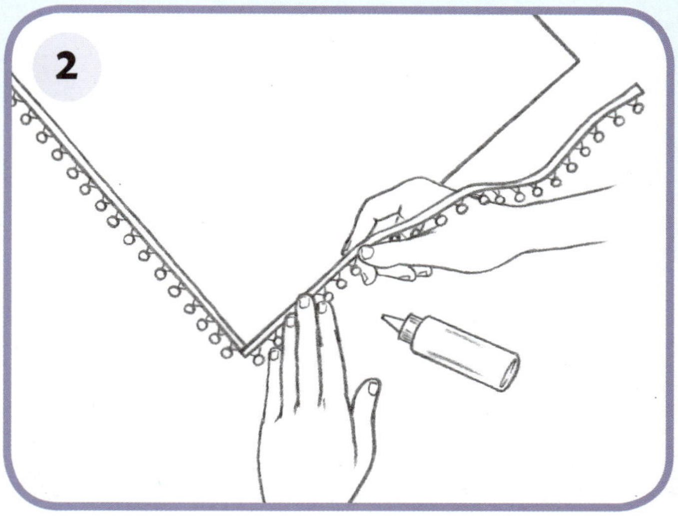

▶ Open up your fabric square and lay it flat. Add trim to its edges using craft glue. Let it dry completely.

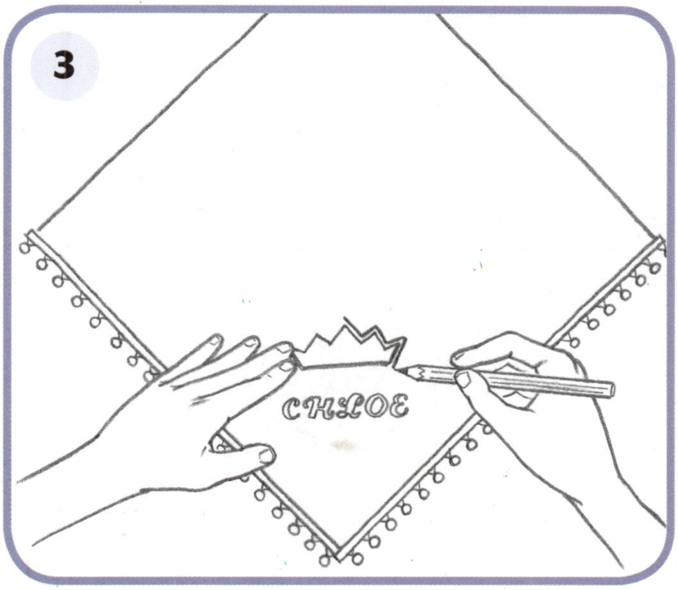

◀ Draw a simple outline of your desired image. Carefully cut out your shape and lightly trace around it onto the bandana. Use a pencil for light-colored fabric and a white pencil or crayon for darker fabrics.

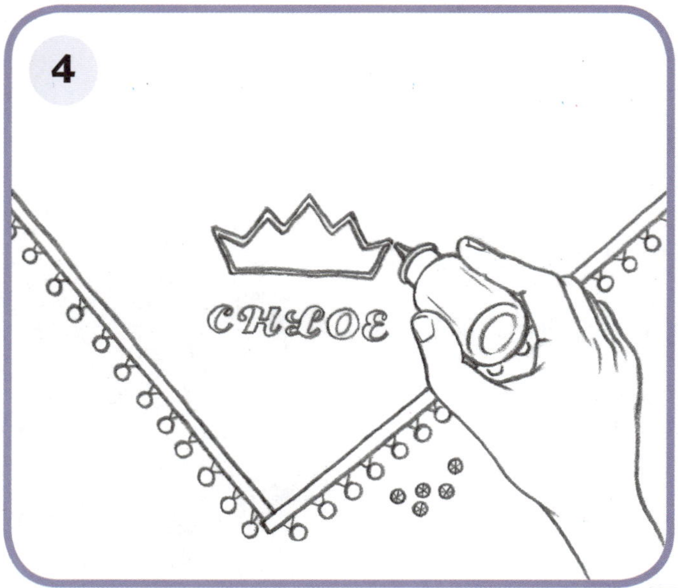

▶ Using fabric paint, carefully paint over the outline that you traced. (You may want to practice on paper before applying the paint to your bandana.) Let it dry completely according to the fabric paint instructions. If you wish, adorn your design with jewels.

Baking Fun!

Grab a grown-up to help you make your favorite horse this special treat.

Horse Treats

INGREDIENTS

- 1 shredded carrot
- 1 shredded apple
- 1 cup molasses
- 2½ cups uncooked oats
- 2 tablespoons vegetable oil

DIRECTIONS

1. Have an adult help you with and supervise this project.
2. Preheat your oven to 300 degrees.
3. Mix all the ingredients together in a large bowl.
4. Pour the mixture onto a greased baking tray.
5. Bake the treats for 40 minutes or until golden brown.
6. Cool for four hours in your refrigerator.
7. Roll the mixture into horse-bite-sized balls.

Horses love apples and carrots—even when they aren't baked inside a treat!

Horsing Around!

Grab a pen, pencil, markers, or crayons and get ready to show off your equine pride with these fun activities!

Horse Trivia

Think you know a lot about horses?
Test your knowledge with these trivia questions.

1 How do you know how old a horse is?
   A. You ask it
   B. By how big it is
   C. By looking at its teeth

2 What do you call a male horse?

3 What do you call a female horse?

4 What do you call a baby horse?

5 Horses usually wear...
   A. hats.
   B. shoes.
   C. sweaters.

6 What vegetable is the same size as a horse's brain?
   A. Potato
   B. Pea
   C. Eggplant

7 How many hours does a horse sleep each night?
   A. 8-9
   B. 3-4
   C. Horses never sleep

8 Of the following foods, which one doesn't fit into a horse's diet?
   A. Grass
   B. Radish
   C. Hot dog

9 How can you tell what kind of mood a horse is in?

A. By the way it walks
B. By its facial expressions
C. Horses don't have feelings

10 Do horses drink more water than humans?

Horse Trivia Answers

1. **C.**
2. **Stallion**
3. **Mare**
4. **Foal**
5. **B.** (Their shoes are made of metal!)
6. **A.**
7. **B.**
8. **C.** (Horses are herbivores—they don't eat meat.)
9. **B.** (Watching a horse's ears, eyes, and mouth can give you clues about what it's thinking.)
10. **Yes** (They drink up to 10 gallons every day!)

Saddle-Up

Add some razzle-dazzle to this bland saddle!

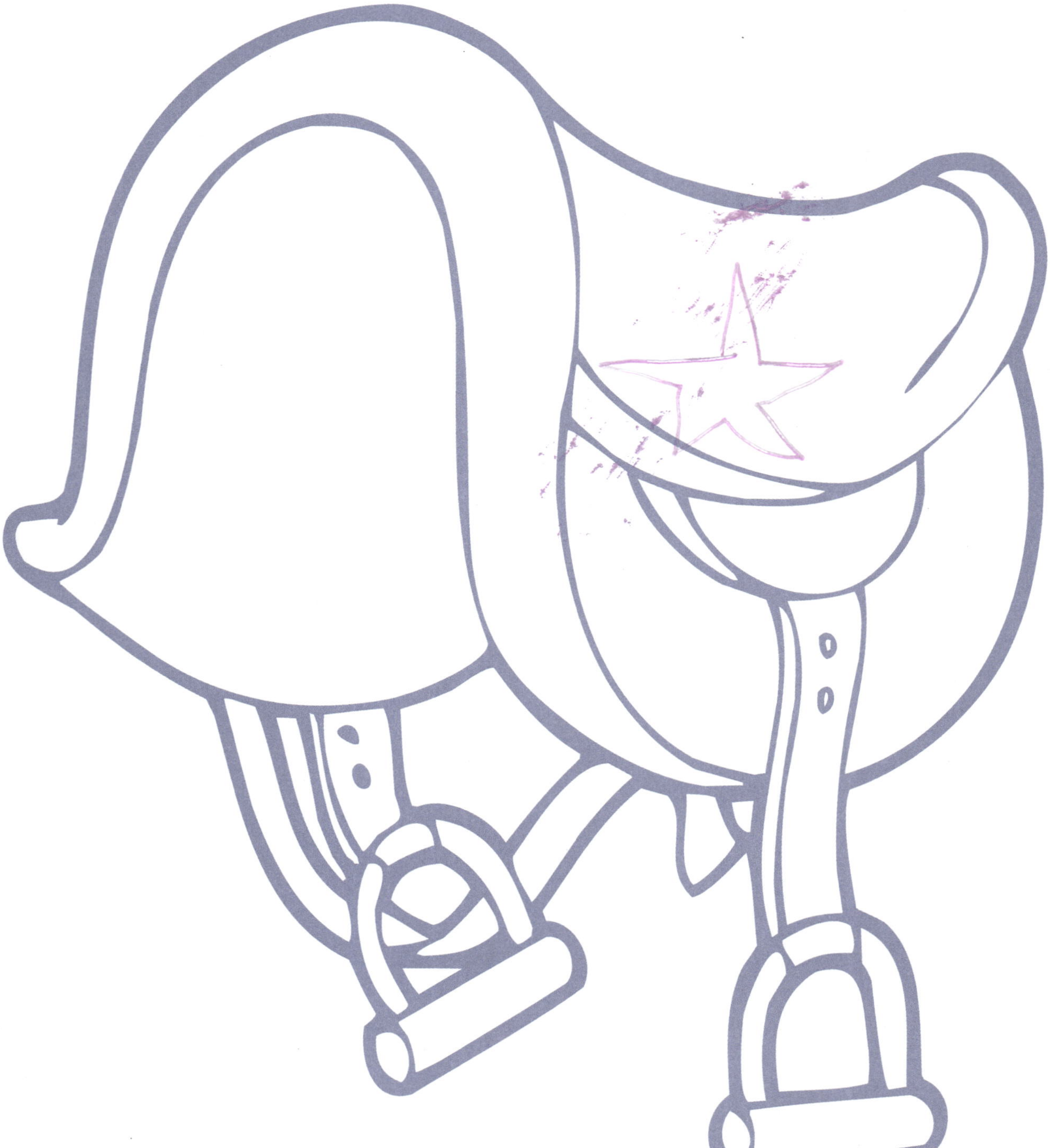

Show Horse

Give this horse a magnificent mane!

Wordsearch

Find and circle the names of different horse breeds hidden in the letters below.

R	O	C	K	Y	M	O	U	N	T	A	I	N	H	O	R	S	E	W	N	A	E	O	E	Q
J	Q	Z	A	P	P	A	L	O	O	S	A	K	C	N	O	K	O	T	A	R	N	Y	V	Y
Z	O	F	O	C	A	E	B	P	A	L	O	M	I	N	O	W	N	R	I	D	X	M	C	Z
U	R	F	M	I	F	R	S	P	N	F	W	Y	L	I	E	D	D	H	N	L	O	L	V	U
T	V	H	U	R	H	I	N	E	L	A	N	D	E	R	M	Q	S	V	I	L	B	S	Q	J
K	F	A	S	Q	D	J	X	R	U	Z	I	U	A	U	D	Q	I	C	U	Y	E	H	E	W
R	X	N	T	F	A	R	A	B	I	A	N	C	G	E	L	C	O	P	K	T	R	E	C	Q
F	Y	O	A	R	S	L	J	H	I	G	H	L	A	N	D	P	O	N	Y	R	L	T	N	Q
C	R	V	N	I	W	I	K	F	D	T	N	N	Y	B	Z	C	A	W	L	F	A	L	D	P
Q	H	E	G	E	I	A	J	Z	S	C	X	P	P	V	N	K	P	R	F	P	N	A	R	Z
U	D	R	L	S	R	Z	I	C	F	P	A	S	O	F	I	N	O	B	Q	R	D	N	Y	J
R	C	I	T	I	L	M	R	W	U	N	G	E	H	V	V	P	I	T	J	P	E	D	J	B
R	U	A	A	A	P	L	I	P	I	Z	Z	A	N	E	R	O	J	W	S	T	R	P	E	G
S	Q	N	Z	N	X	D	G	T	D	Z	Z	V	E	J	U	Y	I	Q	X	N	N	O	O	T
T	E	N	N	E	S	S	E	E	W	A	L	K	I	N	G	H	O	R	S	E	B	N	T	H
C	O	L	V	L	B	S	C	L	Y	D	E	S	D	A	L	E	H	T	N	E	D	Y	W	Q
A	M	E	R	I	C	A	N	Q	U	A	R	T	E	R	H	O	R	S	E	W	E	R	X	B

Clydesdale
Highland Pony
Nokota
Paso Fino
Shetland Pony

Appaloosa
Friesian
Lipizzaner
Oberlander
Rhinelander

Shire
Arabian
Hanoverian
Mustang
Palomino

Rocky Mountain Horse
Tennessee Walking Horse
American Quarter Horse

Answers on page 96.

Prize Pony Maze

Help this pretty pony get to her hard-earned trophy!

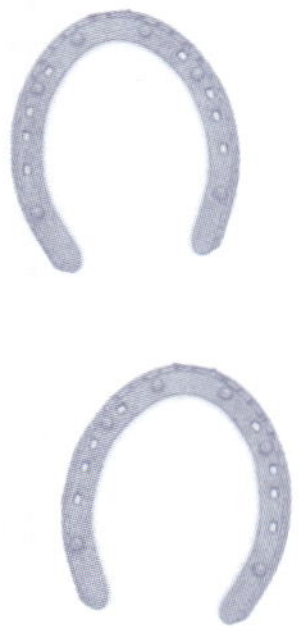

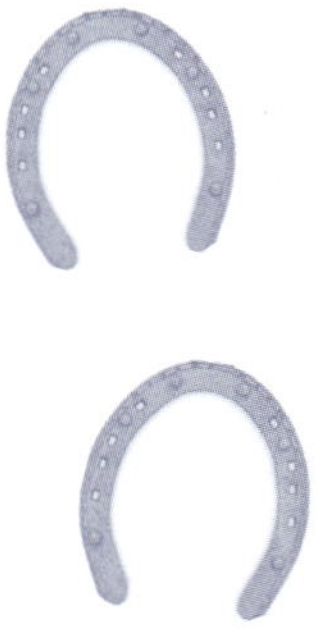

Solution on page 96.

Equine Crossword

Write the answers to the questions in the corresponding squares. Hint: All the answers can be found in this book!

ACROSS

2. This horse has long hairs on its ankles that look like feathers covering its hooves.

3. This horse is also known as the "stepping horse."

8. This pony originated in Scotland.

10. Cowboys prefer this breed.

11. This horse has large eyes, pointed ears, and a dished profile.

12. This is an ancient Austrian breed.

DOWN

1. The Kathiawari is a favorite of ____ ________ athletes.

4. This is the fastest breed of horse.

5. The Pony of the ______ was bred for children to show and ride.

6. This breed has won more World Cups than any other breed.

7. This horse has ears that curve inward.

9. The Tennessee Walking Horse is known for its smooth ______.

Answers on page 96.

I Love Horses! Diary

Strength, speed, sense, and showmanship—
what's not to love about horses?
This diary is the perfect show ring
for you to pony up your thoughts about
these lovable beasts, wild and domestic!

Give 'em a Nuzzle

Favorite horse breeds

Best names for a horse

Most elegant equine coat colors

Coolest famous horses

Favorite horse memory

What I like about horses

Your Horse's Favorite Things

Now write down your horse pal's faves.
(It's okay if your horsey is an imaginary one!)

Most appetizing foods

Yummiest treats

Best ways to pass the time

Favorite trails or tracks

Fave place to be petted (or scratched)

Favorite hangouts

Show Ring

Use these pages to paste in the best horse pictures you can find—they can be of your own or just favorite images you've collected!

To the Races

Now make a collage of equines in action: in the races, the rodeo, the show ring, or even out in the wild! Look in magazines, newspapers, or online to find the clips you need.

Harness Your Creativity

Are you champing at the bit to demonstrate your artistic ability? This is the place to leave your hoof print. Decorate these pages with your horse doodle art.

Horse Tales

Every horse has a tale—or a whole stable full of them! Tell a favorite equine story here, such as the first time you rode a horse or what it's like to attend a show.

Stable Fever

What is it that makes you love horses so much—their gentle way of nuzzling, their elegant stride, their smooth ride? Tell all about your equine passion here.

All About

Name of horse

Birthday

Stabled at

Breed

Color

Nicknames

How/why did you choose your horse's name?

What's so special about this horse?

Hoof Prints

Share more of your favorite horse moments here.

Mane Attraction

Decorate these picture frames and then use tape or glue to attach a picture of your favorite horse!

Horse of a Different Color

Give this horse a colorful coat!

Sketch Pad

Now that you have practiced drawing all your favorite breeds step by step on scrap paper, you can fill the pages of this sketch pad with finished colored drawings. You can even decorate your scenes with the stickers in the back of this book!

Puzzle Answers

Page 54: Wordsearch

R	O	C	K	Y	M	O	U	N	T	A	I	N	H	O	R	S	E	W	N	A	E	O	E	Q
J	Q	Z	A	P	P	A	L	O	O	S	A	K	C	N	O	K	O	T	A	R	N	Y	V	Y
Z	O	F	O	C	A	E	B	P	A	L	O	M	I	N	O	W	N	R	I	D	X	M	C	Z
U	R	F	M	I	F	R	S	P	N	F	W	Y	L	I	E	D	D	H	N	L	O	L	V	U
T	V	H	U	R	H	I	N	E	L	A	N	D	E	R	M	Q	S	V	I	L	B	S	Q	J
K	F	A	S	Q	D	J	X	R	U	Z	I	U	A	U	D	Q	I	C	U	Y	E	H	E	W
R	X	N	T	F	A	R	A	B	I	A	N	C	G	E	L	C	O	P	K	T	R	E	C	Q
F	Y	O	A	R	S	L	J	H	I	G	H	L	A	N	D	P	O	N	Y	R	L	T	N	Q
C	R	V	N	I	W	I	K	F	D	T	N	N	Y	B	Z	C	A	W	L	F	A	L	D	P
Q	H	E	G	E	I	A	J	Z	S	C	X	P	P	V	N	K	P	R	F	P	N	A	R	Z
U	D	R	L	S	R	Z	I	C	F	P	A	S	O	F	I	N	O	B	Q	R	D	N	Y	J
R	C	I	T	I	L	M	R	W	U	N	G	E	H	V	V	P	I	T	J	P	E	D	J	B
R	U	A	A	A	P	L	I	P	I	Z	Z	A	N	E	R	O	J	W	S	T	R	P	E	G
S	Q	N	Z	N	X	D	G	T	D	Z	Z	V	E	J	U	Y	I	Q	X	N	N	O	O	T
T	E	N	N	E	S	S	E	E	W	A	L	K	I	N	G	H	O	R	S	E	B	N	T	H
C	O	L	V	L	B	S	C	L	Y	D	E	S	D	A	L	E	H	T	N	E	D	Y	W	Q
A	M	E	R	I	C	A	N	Q	U	A	R	T	E	R	H	O	R	S	E	W	E	R	X	B

Page 55: Prize Pony Maze

Page 56: Equine Crossword

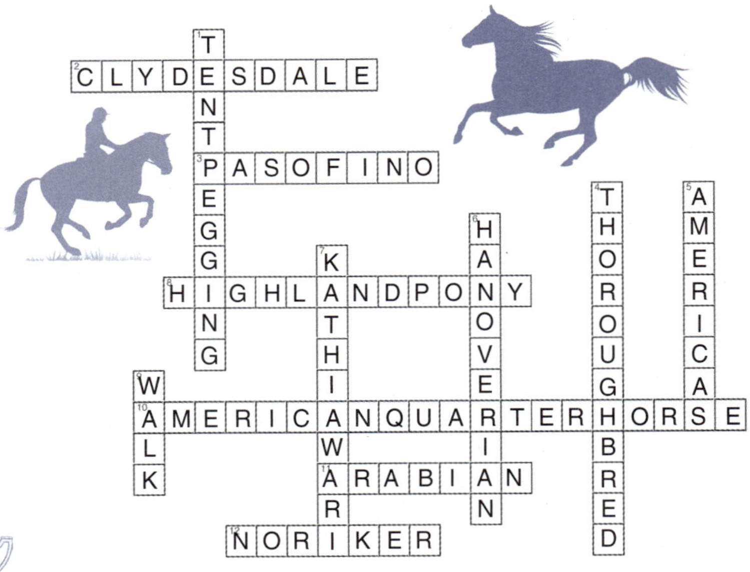

Have an adult help you cut out these equine accessories!

Exercise Good Horse Sense...

Knock First!

Talk to the Hoof!

I love horses!

Hay!

What' cha reading?

Hold Your Horses!

(I'm sleeping!)

Whinny if you love horses!

Have an adult help you cut out these horses—then you can build your own scene!

Fold along the line to make the horse stand up!

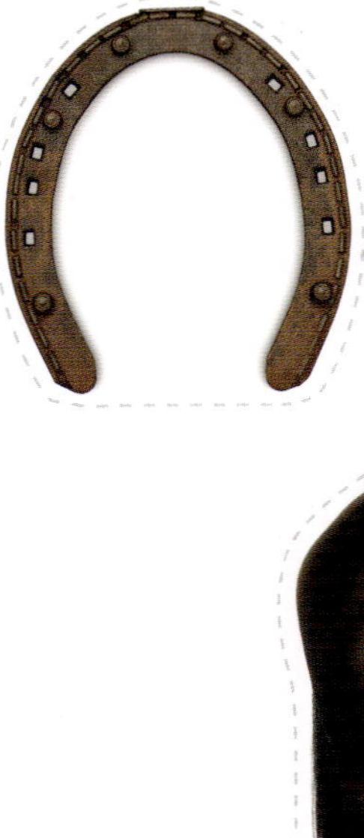

Decorate these postcards and mail them to a friend!

Place
Stamp
Here

Place
Stamp
Here